WHITETAIL

WHITETAIL

ROBERT M. McCLUNG

ILLUSTRATED BY IRENE BRADY

William Morrow and Company, Inc.
New York

2 3 4 5 6 7 8 9 10
Library of Congress Cataloging-in-Publication Data
McClung, Robert M.
Whitetail.
Summary: A fawn is born and grows up, dealing with the
dangers present in nature, learning to avoid cars,
hunters, snowmobiles, and dogs, and occasionally being
aided by a friendly young man.
1. White-tailed deer—Juvenile literature.
2. Wildlife conservation—Juvenile literature.
[1. White-tailed deer. 2. Deer] I. Brady, Irene, ill.
II. Title.
QL737.U55M22 1987   86-18183
ISBN 0-688-06126-5
ISBN 0-688-06127-3 (lib. bdg.)

To Gregory

Contents

WHITETAIL

1

Fawn in the Forest

Pushing through leafy shadows, the doe came to the edge of the forest. She stopped to nibble at several tender sassafras leaves, then walked a few steps into the cleared field ahead. At her back was the big woods, a vast stand of towering pine, hemlock, birch, and mixed hardwoods that stretched upward to a distant high ridge—the summit of Blue Mountain. Beyond it, dim in the morning haze, stretched a whole range of tree-covered slopes. These were the Alleghenies of central Pennsylvania.

The cleared hillside below the forest was a hayfield. Here the air was sweet with the smell of red clover, with honeybees and big yellow swallowtails wandering from blossom to blossom. Below the meadow there were plowed fields and an apple orchard; beyond them stood a big red barn and a white farmhouse.

The doe heard cows bawling faint in the distance, then the shrill bark of a dog. At the sound her big ears twitched nervously. Stepping back into the woods, she headed up the slope. To the east the warm sun of early June was just rising above the treetops.

The past winter had been a hard and hungry one, and the doe was just beginning to regain some of the weight she had lost during the cold months. Her red summer coat was growing in, but a few ragged patches of the faded brown winter coat still clung to her sides and flanks. As she wandered upward, she stopped here and there to crop tender new ferns or to browse on the leafy tips of low branches.

Passing through a thick stand of laurel and hemlock, she came into a small, wild clearing bright with buttercups and daisies. Ahead a sparrow hawk dropped down to seize an unwary field mouse, and a woodchuck whistled at the entrance to its burrow. The doe paid no attention to them.

As she approached a ledge of rock, she heard a faint rattling sound, like the rustle of dried leaves. Instantly alert, she stopped, her ears cocked forward. Just a few feet ahead a big timber rattlesnake was sunning itself.

As the doe came closer, the snake rattled faintly once again, then uncoiled and crawled over to a crack in the rocks. It didn't want a fight. Neither did the doe. If she had felt threatened, she would have attacked the rattler, rearing up and striking at it with her sharp hoofs. Today she merely circled and went on as the snake slithered into the crack in the rock ledge and disappeared.

The doe wanted to find a good spot for the birth of her fawn. The time was very near. So on she went, through another small clearing full of low huckleberry bushes and sumac and again into the big woods, where only fingers of sunlight pierced through the thick branches. At the base of a giant hemlock tree she stopped. The time had come.

The fawn's birth was quick and easy. When it dropped to the ground, it was still partly enveloped in its birth sac. Seizing the membrane and tearing it with her teeth, the doe removed it from her young one. Then she began to lick the newborn fawn, cleaning and scrubbing its wet coat. When she finished, almost none of the fawn's body scent remained. Satisfied at last, she nudged the little one, a male, encouraging him to stand up.

Long legs flopping, the fawn floundered and rolled over as he attempted to rise. At last he got to his foreknees. Unsteadily, he pushed his hind end up, then staggered to his feet. Still wobbling, the fawn nudged along his mother's side until he found her full milk bag. Seizing one of her four teats in his mouth, he tugged vigorously, gulping down the rich, warm milk.

On the day of his birth Star weighed just six pounds. His red coat was sleek and satiny, with a row of small

white spots along each side of the ridge of his back. His sides and upper legs were dappled with irregular white spots as well. His big ears, white inside and red on the outside, were fringed with black, and his huge eyes were a deep blue-brown. In the middle of his forehead was a tiny white blaze.

As soon as he finished nursing, the doe washed Star once more, licking and drying him with her tongue. Then she led him a few steps to a soft bed of dried leaves beside a giant moss-covered log. On one side, a thick stand of laurel shielded the bed from view; on the other side, tall ferns and blossoming clumps of trilliums surrounded the hiding place. Nudging Star into the bed, the doe pushed him down with her moist black nose. This would be the fawn's resting and hiding place until he was old enough to follow his mother.

When Star was settled in his bed, the doe walked away and lay down in a stand of witch hazel and small hemlocks a hundred or so yards away. She could watch over the fawn from this spot and guard him from danger. But she was also far enough away so that her body scent would not lead any enemies to the scentless little one.

With his legs curled beneath him, Star settled down to rest. His spotted coat helped to hide him in his bed. Its red color blended with the dried leaves of the forest floor, and the white markings seemed part of the dancing spots of sunlight that marked the leaves and branches around him.

Star remained in this hiding place for almost a week, seldom venturing more than a few feet away from it unless his mother was with him. He nursed half a dozen times or more each day; then he often slept while his mother wandered off to gather food for herself. At other times he lay in his bed and watched the forest life around him.

Above him a nuthatch probed for insects in the bark of a white pine tree, and a red-headed woodpecker hammered on the trunk of a dead birch. Sitting on a low branch, a red squirrel flicked its tail up and down and scolded a chipmunk that lived under the big log. Once a tiny shrew scampered across one edge of Star's bed, searching for insects.

Danger threatened one evening when his mother was away foraging in a nearby clearing. A hungry bobcat passed by, just a few feet from the fawn's bed. Star lay perfectly still, his head and neck stretched out flat on the leaves beneath him. The big cat did not notice him.

Later that evening a mother skunk and her four young ones shuffled toward the log. Snuffing noisily, the mother skunk began to dig for beetle grubs in the rotting wood. One of the young skunks walked over to Star and sniffed at him. Curious, the fawn sniffed back. The mother skunk glanced at them and grunted sharply.

Turning, the little skunk scurried back to her. After a few minutes the family traveled on.

As night came, Star snuggled into his leaf bed and slept. An owl called in the warm darkness, and wood mice skittered through the dried leaves around him.

When he was two weeks old, Star weighed twelve pounds, twice as much as on the day of his birth. Now he began to wander about on his own. His mother could easily find him, however, for glands between his split hoofs gave off a scent that she could follow. When she located him, she would nudge him with her nose and guide him back to the spot where she had left him.

One afternoon, while Star nursed, the doe heard noises

from the wooded slope below them. First came the shuffling sound of dried leaves, then the crack of a dead branch. Something was coming. Pushing the fawn down, the doe stood tense, her big ears pricked forward to catch the slightest sound, her dark eyes staring ahead to catch any movement.

Another limb snapped, and not far away a dog barked. A moment later a small black-and-white dog appeared, and then a boy. They were no more than seventy-five yards away.

The doe bounded away from Star with a tremendous leap just as the dog spotted her. Yelping with excitement, he took off after her. When she had run about fifty yards, well away from the fawn, Star's mother stopped. Whirling about, she stared at the little dog running toward her and snorted. She stamped her feet and took off again, her tail raised, its snowy underside waving from side to side like a white banner. She was trying to lead the dog and the boy away from Star. The dog ran after her as fast as he could go.

"Ben, come back here!" the boy called. "Back!"

At the order the dog hesitated, then stopped and gazed back at his master. Turning, he looked ahead to the spot where the doe had stopped once again. "Come here, Ben," the boy ordered firmly. Reluctantly the pet turned and headed toward his master.

The doe stamped her feet again, then bounded into

the underbrush and disappeared. The twelve-year-old boy watched her go. Sam lived on the farm in the valley and had been seeing deer ever since he could remember. By now he knew quite a bit about them. From her behavior he suspected that the doe had a fawn hidden somewhere nearby.

As the dog returned to him, the farm boy saw the doe circling back toward them. She snorted and stamped once more, then bounded away. She was still trying to lure them into following her. But Sam was not fooled. He fastened a piece of rope around Ben's neck and walked on the way he had come.

Sam searched for the fawn for a good fifteen minutes but couldn't find it. Giving up, he started back toward home and almost stumbled on Star, who had lain motionless on his bed ever since his mother had left him. Just several feet apart, the boy, the dog, and the fawn stared at one another.

The sheep dog strained at the rope, eager to go up and sniff at the little deer, but the boy held him back. "No, Ben, leave it alone!" he cautioned. Sam looked at the fawn and marveled at its perfection. He saw the white, star-shaped blaze on its forehead. He had never seen a deer with such a mark. He'd know this one if he saw it again.

Backing slowly away, Sam headed for home. The doe had been trying to lead him away from her fawn,

just as he suspected. Well, he and Ben wouldn't hurt it.

After they had gone, Star's mother came silently through the forest and stood by her fawn. She sniffed and nudged him, then let him nurse. That evening she led him away from the old hiding place and took him to a new spot farther up the slope. Star would soon be old enough to accompany her on her wanderings.

2

Summer Days

By early July, Star weighed twenty-five pounds, four times as much as he had weighed at birth. He was strong and active and could run almost as fast as his mother. Now he began to follow her wherever she went. While she cropped the lush summer greenery, Star walked beside her and examined the life around him.

He sniffed at leaves and flowers and sometimes sampled them. At first he jumped at every moving shadow: a leaf tossing in the breeze, a toad hopping across the path, a bird flying overhead. But he soon grew used to the ordinary sights and sounds and smells of the forest. Every day he became more experienced in the ways of life in the woods.

At dawn he would listen to the first sleepy birdsongs or watch a skunk shuffle past, heading for its daytime hiding place. During the day he often heard catbirds or mourning doves calling from their nests in the thick undergrowth at the edge of the forest.

One morning a yearling female deer joined Star and his mother. This was Star's older sister, one of the twin fawns his mother had given birth to the year before. The other, a yearling buck, did not rejoin them. Instead, he and several other young male deer banded together for the summer.

After her first fawn a doe usually has twins. If the doe is old, however, or if the winter has been unusually severe, with little available food, she may bear just one fawn.

Star, his mother, and his sister roamed their range together during the hot summer days. Several other does and their fawns often joined them. The deer wandered through the woodlands together, the older deer taking a mouthful of leaves here, a nibble there, snipping off each morsel between their lower front teeth and the horny pad like a scrubbing board in the roof of the mouth. The fawns pranced and played beside them, sniffing at woodland plants and sampling buds. When they were hungry, they ran to their mothers to nurse.

The deer were usually active from just before dawn until midmorning. During the heat of the day they would lie in some cool and sheltered spot, hidden in a thicket of low-branched trees and bushes. In the late afternoon they would once again venture forth in search of food.

After she had eaten enough, Star's mother would lie down. Coughing up a cud of plants she had just eaten, she would chew it with regular cross movements of her jaws, crushing the rough plant fibers between her rear grinding teeth, or molars. After the mouthful was well chewed, she would swallow it and cough up another cud.

While the older deer rested and chewed their cuds, the fawns would play with one another. Star would jump at first one playmate, then another. Sometimes he ran in circles around a fawn or chased it. Tossing his head, he would leap at another and butt it, trying to knock it over. He and the others occasionally chased butterflies or big grasshoppers that flew up beneath their hoofs on crackling yellow-and-black wings.

Before dawn one morning the does and the fawns came to a clearing below the big woods. Jumping over a low, split-rail fence, they ventured into the pasture-land beyond to browse on the grasses and ferns that grew there. Partway down the hillside Star could see a number of huge black-and-white animals. He heard low mooing sounds and then loud bawling. The farmer's cows were grazing in the field.

Star's mother and the other does did not seem to be alarmed by the cows, so Star was not afraid either. He walked toward the cattle, curious to see them at close range. Several of the big, broad-muzzled cows raised their heads to stare at him. One calf, just as curious as he, ambled toward him. The two young animals touched noses; then Star jumped back and ran to his mother. The calf stared after him, then kicked up its heels and ran back to its mother as well.

Late one afternoon the old doe led Star and his sister to a pond—really a small lake formed by the damming of the lowland creek by a beaver family. Near one shore was the big beaver lodge, a huge mound of branches rising above the water. Beyond it was the long, low

beaver dam, formed of intertwined sticks and branches, plastered with mud.

Dragonflies cruised back and forth across the water on glittering wings, and Star could hear the deep *chug-o-rum* of bullfrogs. He watched a mother wood duck and her family of fluffy brown ducklings as they zigged and zagged through the reeds. As the fawn waded into the pond to drink beside his mother, he heard the sharp slap of a beaver's tail as it slipped into the water. On the far shore, a whippoorwill was calling.

The deer came to this pond often, usually in the late afternoon or early evening. Sometimes Star would see the beavers gnawing at trees or carrying branches for their dam. He often saw a mother raccoon and her young fishing for frogs or tadpoles in the shallows. Once he saw a big buck deer when he came to drink. His widespread antlers were covered with velvet.

At dusk bats and swifts zoomed and fluttered above the water, chasing mosquitoes and moths and other night insects. As darkness came, fireflies glowed like tiny lanterns rising and falling above the water. The pond was a place where many animals lived or came to drink or find food.

One evening, as Star drank at the edge of the pond, he saw a canoe coming around a wooded point. He watched wide-eyed as it came closer. It was paddled by Sam. He had been fishing. When he spotted the deer on the bank, the boy stopped paddling and sat motionless, watching them. As the canoe drifted closer, he recognized the fawn with the tiny white star. This was the one he'd seen in the forest just a few weeks ago!

Star's mother snorted, then wheeled around and bounded away. Star and his sister followed.

During these warm, lazy evenings of late summer the deer sometimes visited patches of blackberries to feed on the ripening fruit. One night, in their search for food, they ventured close to the road that wound through the valley. At one point, where blackberries grew thick at the edge of the forest, the bushes came right to the roadside.

As Star munched on the juicy berries, he heard a strange sound. He saw two great yellow eyes approaching. The nearer they got, the larger and brighter they became. A car was approaching. The sound of the motor rose to a roar, and Star was dazzled by the blinding glare of the headlights.

After a moment of hesitation his mother dashed across the road in front of the speeding car. Star followed, close behind her. Both of them reached the opposite side in safety, but the yearling doe was not so fortunate. Confused by the bright lights, she had hesitated a moment too long. As she bounded after her mother,

she crashed into the front of the car and was thrown twenty feet. She was dead before she hit the ground.

The car careened wildly to one side, then crashed into a guardrail beside the road. Its fender was crumpled, and the headlights, radiator, and windshield were shattered. Dazed and bewildered by the sudden collision, the driver opened the car door and staggered out. He was not seriously injured, but his face was cut and bleeding from flying glass. In a few moments another car stopped to help him.

Far up the opposite slope Star and his mother turned to look back. The yearling doe did not join them. After a moment they ran on.

3

Moon of Falling Leaves

By mid-August Star weighed nearly thirty-five pounds. He was eating plenty of plant food now, but he still nursed when his mother would let him. His heavy winter coat was starting to grow in, and his babyhood spots were slowly fading. Star was growing up.

Chicory and Queen Anne's lace bloomed in the bright September meadows, and clumps of goldenrod and purple asters brightened the open hillsides. As he browsed in a clearing one sunny afternoon, Star saw many big black and orange-brown butterflies flying past. These were monarch butterflies, starting their long trip south for the winter.

When October came, the sugar maples flamed red and yellow, and birches gleamed like gold against the dark green of the hemlocks. V-shaped flights of Canada geese flew overhead. As the fall days grew shorter, crickets chirped their warnings of cold weather to come.

All the animals that would remain in the northern forests were making their preparations for the hard months ahead. Some built snug winter homes. Others collected and stored caches of provisions. Most of them stuffed themselves with food every day as though they could never get enough to eat.

Star and his mother feasted on the fall harvest, too. Every day they competed with the squirrels for acorns and nuts in the forest. On moonlit nights they ventured down the slopes to eat apples that had dropped in the orchards or to munch on dried kernels of corn in fields where the rustling brown rows of corn still stood. They wandered through the woodlands, searching for mushrooms, and ate their fill of leaves and buds as well. Like all the other animals, they were storing up layers of fat to help tide them over the winter.

In late October heavy frosts coated the meadows and clearings with silver. Leaves swirled down in showers of yellow and brown, orange and red. This was the time when big antlered bucks, eager to mate, began to follow does. The time of the rut—the breeding season—was starting. The male deer had antlers that were polished and sharp, and Star sometimes heard the clash of these weapons as two bucks fought each other for the right to mate with a receptive doe. To the five-month-old fawn the bucks looked like giants. They were short-tempered and ready for a fight. Star stayed well away from any of them that attempted to approach his mother.

Star's mother was still not ready to mate. She avoided eager males whenever she could and ran away from any buck that was too persistent. One day in November, however, she allowed a big buck to come up to her and nuzzle her side. She was ready to accept him. The big buck stayed with them all that day, and in the evening he mated with the doe. By the next morning her brief period of being receptive had passed, and the doe had lost interest in him. But the mating had been successful. If all went well, she would bear his fawns the next June. Rejected, the buck wandered off to seek other mates.

A few days later Star and his mother saw a man on the slope below the woods. He was crossing an open meadow, carrying a longbow—a modern version of the bows that woodland Indians had used as hunting weapons during pioneer days and before. At the man's side was a quiver full of arrows. The season for deer hunting had started that morning, and bow hunting was allowed for a few days before the shotgun and rifle season.

Hidden in the trees, Star and his mother watched as the hunter approached the edge of the forest. The doe bounded silently into the woodland, and Star followed. His mother knew from previous experience that at this

season of the year it was best to keep as much distance as possible between human beings and herself.

They did not see the bow hunter again, but that evening they came upon the big buck that had mated with Star's mother. He was lying under a clump of heavy bushes near the edge of the orchard, his side stained with blood. His tongue hung out, and he was panting heavily. Just behind his right shoulder the feathered end of an arrow was sticking out of his side. The steel arrowhead was buried in his lung.

When the hunter had shot him, the buck had bounded away and escaped through the woods. He had traveled more than a mile before he had finally dropped. The hunter had not found him. Now, with every breath he took, bright, foamy blood bubbled out of his mouth and nostrils. He would soon die.

A few days later Sam and his father found the dead buck as they walked up the slope to mark several trees to be cut for winter firewood. The farm boy looked at the fallen deer and shook his head sadly. That buck had been proud and beautiful and full of life just a short time ago.

Sam had already decided that he liked wild things better alive than dead. He knew that many farm animals—pigs, sheep, and calves—ended up being killed for food. His father raised animals for their meat, and the boy ate ham or bacon or veal nearly every day.

Indians and pioneers and some modern-day people hunted to get meat for their families, too. But the hunter who had shot this buck had not needed to kill for food. He killed just for the sport of it. He had fatally wounded the deer and then let him get away. The big buck had died for nothing.

On the other hand, Sam realized that in this area wolves and mountain lions—the deer's natural enemies—had been killed off by humans long ago. And wildlife specialists said that if hunters did not take their toll of deer, helping to keep the population in balance, many of the deer would starve to death during hard winters. There would not be enough food for all of them.

Star and his mother kept to the deepest part of the forest when the rifle and shotgun hunting season began soon afterward. They heard the sound of gunfire many times during the next few days, as hunters roamed the countryside. Many deer were killed in the region during the ten-day hunting season, but Star and his mother escaped.

4

Winter Woods

The winter's first snowfall started at dusk one evening in mid-December. Star watched the soft white flakes drift silently downward, sprinkling the forest floor with white. He and his mother lay in a bed of dried leaves, sheltered overhead with laurel and overhanging hemlock branches. They were snug and warm.

The snow ended during the night, and only a couple of inches covered the ground. Shaking the white flakes from their backs, Star and his mother left their beds at dawn to look for food. Their heavy winter coats had protected them from the clinging layers of snow. Each deer had a thick, dense undercoat of soft hair, overlaid with an insulating outer coat of coarse, wiry hairs that were hollow.

Star sniffed at the snow as he walked through it. He licked up a few mouthfuls, then scuffed his hoofs in it, watching it scatter in powdery flakes. Other animals had gone through the snow before him. One set of tracks showed where a snowshoe hare had hopped past. A few feet away a gray squirrel had left smaller tracks as it foraged for acorns hidden under the snow. At one spot tiny, feathery tracks zigzagged back and forth, then ended abruptly. A small spot of blood and the fan marks of wings brushing the snow showed where an owl had swooped down to seize a mouse. Later in the winter, as the snow became deeper and more packed, mice would make tunnels under the snow. These hidden runways would give them protection from foxes and owls; they would be convenient, safe pathways in which

the mice could travel as they searched for seeds and roots and other food.

Now that snow blanketed the ground, Star found that getting food was not as easy as it had been during the fall. Following his mother's example, he used his hoofs to scrape the snow away to search for acorns and plants hidden under the white flakes. Most of the time he and his mother got enough to eat by cropping buds and twigs at the tips of bare branches or browsing on cedar and other evergreens.

Several other snowfalls soon followed, and by early January a white blanket nearly eight inches deep covered the woodland. Before the drifts became any deeper, Star and his mother joined a number of other deer in a sheltered valley, several miles from their summer area. The valley had a thick tangle of low trees and evergreens, and food was comparatively easy to get. The deer spent much of their time on a southern-facing slope, where the snow was not as deep as in many other areas.

The bucks had dropped their antlers by this time, and with their bony weapons gone, they were very different creatures from the proud and arrogant fighters they had been during the breeding season, just a few weeks before. Many of them took second place to experienced old does and waited meekly for them to feed at a favored spot before pushing in for their share.

So far the winter had been quite mild. February was colder than January, but little snow fell. One afternoon Star and his mother heard a strange, roaring sound in the distance. It was faint at first; then it rose and fell and began to grow steadily stronger. A few moments later Star saw a long, low machine speeding across an open meadow below the wooded slope. The machine was a snowmobile, with a man driving it. It swerved back and forth across the field, then turned sharply and headed up the hill toward the edge of the woodland where Star and his mother were watching. The driver had seen them.

The two deer started to run, but as they leaped away, Star tripped on a fallen limb and fell in a heap in the soft snow. As he struggled to regain his footing, the snowmobile roared past him, very close, then swerved away. The driver laughed and waved. The man thought it was good sport to chase the deer.

Star's mother was bounding into the woods as the snowmobile circled and headed back toward them. But Star was still floundering in the snowdrift as the machine roared past him a second time.

After that sweep the snowmobile driver tired of his play and headed back down the slope. Behind him the machine left a weaving path of packed snow. In the days to come, cross-country skiers would use those paths

to travel through the backcountry. So would domestic dogs.

The dogs came early one morning. Star and his mother heard barking in the distance, and their ears pricked up as the sounds came nearer. Then they saw the dogs running along one of the snowmobile paths. There were four of them: two tawny shepherd dogs as big as wolves, a spotted short-haired hound, and a black mongrel with long hair. When the dogs spotted Star and his mother, they swept forward, baying with excitement. If they could catch up with them, they would attack and kill the deer.

Bounding ahead with tremendous leaps, Star and his mother soon reached the wooded slope where the snow was thinner than in the valley. Here the going was easier for them, and they soon left the dogs behind. The barking grew fainter, and finally they could no longer hear it. The dogs had abandoned the chase.

In late March the weather became much milder. The snow cover receded steadily, and the branches of the oaks and maples took on soft colors as their buds began to swell. Once again patches of green appeared in the woods and open fields. Soon the shrill piping notes of spring peepers sounded from the shallow waters of the pond. Redwings swayed on the reeds along the shore and sang their territorial song.

Star's forehead tingled as two knobs over his eyes began to swell and push upward. Spring was on the way, and his first antlers were beginning to grow. Star was a yearling now.

5

Spike Buck

The mild winter had been kind to the deer, and most of them came through the cold months in good shape. Now it was April; seeds were sprouting, and buds burst into tender green leaves everywhere. The deer had plenty of food. The does were healthy and vigorous; there would be a great many fawns born this spring.

Star was almost a year old now and weighed a hundred pounds. Every day his weight increased as he filled up on spring greenery. His winter coat became patchy, and his red summer coat began to grow in. The swelling velvet-covered knobs on his forehead pushed steadily upward. They would become his first antlers—single spikes.

As antlers grow, they are covered with a soft, hairy skin called velvet. Blood vessels in the velvet bring oxygen and food to the growing antlers, which are bone tissue.

Week after week, Star's spike antlers became longer.

At the same time the older bucks were growing branched antlers. Some of the big bucks had a number of points, or tines, thrusting upward from the main beams of their antlers. Many people believe that they can tell how old a buck is by the number of points it has—one point on each antler for each year of its age. Sometimes this is so, but frequently it isn't. Many young bucks approaching their prime grow antlers with more than the average number of points; bucks past their prime often have fewer points. Much depends upon the buck's general health and vigor and the available food. An examination of a deer's teeth is the most reliable indication of its age.

In May, Star's mother often left him and went off to feed and rest by herself. When Star attempted to follow her, she would turn impatiently and butt him with her head, pushing him away. He was old enough to be on his own, and now there was no place in her life for a spike buck, even her own yearling son. She would soon have new fawns to look after. In early June Star finally left his mother for good. This is usual with yearling bucks; female yearlings, on the other hand, often rejoin their mothers after the older does' newborn fawns are strong enough to travel.

Other spike bucks were receiving the same treatment from their mothers as Star had gotten. He joined two yearling bucks that had been in the winter group with

him. The three young deer wandered through the spring woodlands together, browsing on tender leaves and cropping plant food wherever they went. They fed together before daybreak, in the evening hours after sunset, and sometimes for an hour or two at night. During daylight hours they usually rested, shaded from the hot summer sun and hidden from view by a shelter of heavy brush.

One of the young bucks' favorite places for cooling off and drinking was the beaver pond. Sometimes the deer would see a great blue heron stalking through the shallows as it hunted for frogs and fish. In the warm twilight little brown bats flitted across the darkening water, pursuing insects. One afternoon Star saw the farm boy again, fishing from his canoe. The beaver pond was one of Sam's favorite spots, too.

One day a big black dog surprised Star and the other deer as they waded along the shore. Baying with excitement, the dog leaped into the water and started after them. Two of the young deer splashed ashore and bounded away, but Star was out too far from the bank. As the dog swam toward him, he waded quickly into deeper water and started swimming for the far side of the pond. He kicked out strongly, leaving a rippling furrow of water behind him. But the dog was a strong swimmer, too. He gradually gained on Star as the two of them approached the center of the pond.

Near the far shore a canoe suddenly appeared from behind a thick stand of cattails. Sam had been fishing in a tiny inlet. He had heard the dog barking and had paddled out to investigate. As soon as he saw Star and the big black dog swimming after him, Sam started paddling toward them as fast as he could go.

It took him only a few moments to maneuver his canoe into the open water between the two animals. Waving his paddle in the air, he shouted at the dog. Confused by the sudden interruption, the big black animal swerved away. At almost the same time Star gained the other shore. Scrambling out of the water, he took off through the woods.

Sam watched with satisfaction as the spike buck with the distinctive white blaze on his forehead disappeared. The big dog had already turned and was swimming back toward the shore from which he had come. He was giving up the chase.

Late one evening Star came to the pond by himself. Only a few stars gleamed overhead, and there was no moon. While he was drinking, a glaring white light suddenly shone in his face from the opposite shore, blinding him. A shot rang out, and buckshot whistled over his head. As Star turned and leaped away, a second shot rang out. It missed him, too. In a few seconds he was deep in the woods, out of range of the guns and blinding light.

Poachers—illegal hunters—had fired at him. Unlawful hunters such as these kill many deer every year. These poachers were hunting deer out of season, and they had tried to blind Star with a powerful light. A deer is confused by such a light and does not know how to escape it. This method of hunting deer is illegal, even during the regular hunting season.

One evening in late August, Star and his companions were feeding in a hillside clearing. The weather was sultry, and black clouds towered in the western sky. The deer heard low rumblings of thunder from the clouds, then saw brilliant flashes of lightning that flickered above the distant hills. Suddenly there was a loud clap of thunder, like the firing of many cannons. Heat lightning rippled silently across the sky, and big drops of rain began to fall, making plopping noises as they hit the ground.

A blinding bolt of lightning crackled down from a towering thunderhead, and Star heard a loud clap as the lightning struck a big white oak tree nearby. The great tree split, and half of it fell with an earthshaking crash, nearly hitting one of Star's companions. All of them bounded away and took shelter in the big woods.

The thunderstorm passed, but rain began to fall again the next morning. The downfall increased during the day, and the wind steadily became stronger and more violent. The treetops swayed and creaked above Star, and the roar of the wind sounded everywhere.

Heading into the thickest part of the forest, Star crawled into a stand of laurel bushes and lay down beside a huge log that sheltered him from the worst of the driving wind. All around him the gale sounded with a great roaring through the forest. Above him branches swayed and broke. Star heard loud cracks as one big tree after another crashed to the ground. The storm continued for most of the night. Sheltered by the log and the branches above him, Star was not harmed.

By dawn the wind had died down, and the great storm had finally passed. Star left his bed and walked cautiously through the battered forest. The woods seemed strangely silent, and he had to make his way around one fallen forest giant after another. The rays of the morning sun sparkled on the wet leaves and branches stripped from the trees. In one place a young buck lay dead. Its back had been broken by a huge limb that had fallen on it.

By early September Star's antlers had stopped growing and the velvet had dried. He cleaned the straight, six-inch spikes by scraping them against rough tree trunks and branches. The velvet came off in tattered

shreds, and within two days the sharp spikes of bare bone were clean.

A year and a half old that second fall of his life, Star was a solid 150-pound spike buck. He would not reach his full strength and growth until his fifth or sixth year, but even now he felt the power in his young body, the excitement of the rutting season. He dueled with other young bucks, practicing for the years ahead. He was still too young and inexperienced to challenge any of the older bucks that were now looking for mates. They sent him running with merely a short rush or a baleful stare, their spreading racks of antlers thrust toward him.

When the hunting season opened, many hunters wandered through the Pennsylvania woodlands. The number of deer in the Blue Mountain region was high that fall, for the population had been increasing steadily for several years. The past winter had been quite mild, with plenty of available food. As a result, a high percentage of adult deer had survived, and the does had given birth to many fawns.

State wildlife officials said that there were too many deer in the region for the habitat to support. So they decided that more deer than usual should be shot during this hunting season in order to bring the herd back into balance with the available food and living space. As a result, regulations this fall permitted both bucks and does to be taken.

For ten days Star heard the sound of frequent shots. He had to hide or run several times to avoid being fired at by hunters. Many deer were killed during the hunting season, but Star escaped. By the time the season ended, winter had almost arrived. By all signs it promised to be a hard one.

6

Starvation Time

All the animals of the fields and forests were acting as though they sensed the approaching winter would be a long and severe one. Woodchucks, their sides rolling with fat, had long since retired to their underground burrows. They would sleep the cold months away in deep hibernation. Gray squirrels had built thick-walled leaf nests high in the treetops or prepared snug homes in hollow trees.

The summer birds had flown south. The ones that remained were used to scouring the winter countryside for food. Those scavengers, the crows, cawed in the treetops. Blue jays called to one another in the lower branches. Downy woodpeckers hammered on dead limbs, searching for grubs.

From first light until dark, squirrels, wild turkeys, bears, and many other woodland animals vied with one another in eating and gathering acorns and whatever other foods they found. Red squirrels hid huge stores of nuts and pinecones in sheltered places for future use. Gray squirrels buried countless acorns throughout the forest. They would search for them and dig them up for food as needed during the cold months.

Along with all the other animals, Star filled up on acorns and other nuts. His body was storing layers of fat that would help tide him through the long, cold time ahead. His winter coat, a soft gray-brown, had grown in thick and warm.

The season's first snowfall came in mid-November that year, and by the dawn of the new year a layer of white nearly a foot deep covered the countryside. During the times of heavy snowfall Star would nest down in a leafy bed under low-hanging branches of hemlock. Heavy layers of snow would gather on the evergreen boughs above him, and the branches would sweep low over his head, forming a sheltering roof.

Star would stay in his bed, snug and warm, waiting for the snowfall to end. Then he would roam through the woodland to forage on twigs and leaf buds or wander down to the open fields and paw through the snow, looking for buried clumps of grass or a few frozen potatoes that had been left behind in the farmer's potato field.

More snow fell in early January, and Star soon found it too deep to travel through without difficulty. It was then that he and other deer in the area gathered together in a nearby sheltered valley, close to the winding creek that fed the frozen beaver pond. Such a place, where deer sometimes stay during the winter months, is called a yard. In the yard there were many cedar trees as well as a good supply of alder and other shrubby underbrush. The deer kept close to the available food and tramped out many crisscrossing trails through the area from one group of trees to another.

Later in the month even more snow fell. Soon the drifts were more than two feet deep in many places—too deep for Star or the other deer to make their way through. Now the movements of all of them were restricted to the paths that the adult bucks and does had pushed through a few weeks before. The deer used these paths daily and kept them open.

By the end of January the heavy snows had totally imprisoned the deer in their yard. To add to their difficulties, temperatures plunged to zero and below. The deer moved about as little as possible in the frigid air, for they needed to conserve their energy and body heat as much as possible. Star usually remained in his bed most of the day and night, except when he was forced to venture out to hunt for food. Like all the other deer, he was finding it more and more difficult to find enough to eat.

Most of the available buds and tender twigs had long since been stripped off the trees and eaten. Day after

day the deer had to stretch higher to reach the available food. The big adult deer sometimes stood on their hind legs to browse from high branches that Star and the other yearlings could not reach. The fawns of the year were having the hardest time getting anything to eat.

February—the starvation month—dawned. Icy winds whistled across the countryside, and the whole region suffered a deep freeze as temperatures plunged far below zero. In the forest frozen tree trunks cracked and split with sounds like gunshots. The fawns' ribs showed through their sides as they used up more and more body fat each day. Starving and exhausted, a number of them dropped in their tracks, unable to stand up any longer. Within hours they died. The hard winter was taking its toll.

During this time of starvation the biggest and strongest deer chased the smaller and weaker ones away from the best remaining feeding sites until they had eaten whatever they could find. Star competed with the other yearlings and the old deer for the few patches of possible food that remained—trees and shrubs already picked over by the bigger and stronger deer. In the background a couple of starving fawns often watched, their eyes dull and almost unseeing.

In mid-February a three-day blizzard sealed the fate of a number of the deer that were already weakened from lack of food. Star's mother and her nine-month-old fawn were among the victims. Under such harsh conditions as these it is usually the old and the very young deer that suffer the most.

After the storm the cold remained almost as bitter as ever, but there were a few days of bright sunshine. The top layer of snow melted under the bright noon sun, then froze into a hard, shiny crust during the hours of darkness. Some of the deer, finding that they could walk on the crust, attempted to reach new food areas. Star was one of these.

Advancing cautiously, he made his way over the snow to a clump of red maples near the edge of the beaver pond. He cropped the twigs eagerly and for the first time in weeks nearly filled his belly.

While he ate, a great white owl flew past him. The owl was searching for food, too. Hunger had driven it to this area from its far northern homeland, where the mice and lemmings that were its main food had disappeared. Throughout the north, cold and hunger and disease were taking their toll of many animals.

As Star browsed, he suddenly felt a weight crashing onto his back, knocking him to the ground. A big bobcat was clawing and biting at his neck and shoulders. Thrashing the air with his legs, Star bucked and rolled over, knocking the cat off his back. The snow crust had broken under him, but after floundering for a moment, Star scrambled to his feet. His side and neck

were bleeding from claw and tooth marks, but he was not seriously hurt. The bobcat sprang at him once again, snarling and spitting, but Star struck out with his hoofs and knocked the meat eater away a second time.

Head lowered, he faced his foe, ready to fight for his life. The bobcat hesitated for a moment, its ears laid back and its long canine teeth showing in a snarl. Then it bounded away and disappeared into the woods. Star had proved too much of a fighter for it. Bobcats seldom attack any deer larger than newborn fawns, but this one, driven by hunger, had tried.

As he headed back to the deeryard, Star broke through the crust that had been softened by the sun. He had to struggle hard to clamber out and was breathing heavily by the time he reached one of the trails. Along the way he passed an old deer that had also broken through the crust. It did not have the strength to get out and would die in the drifts.

A few days later Star and several of the other deer in the yard discovered a fresh-cut pile of swamp maple and red cedar branches piled up beside one of their trails. They began to browse eagerly. Soon other deer came to feed as well.

Hidden in the nearby woods, Sam watched with satisfaction. The farm boy had known where the deer were wintering and realized that many of them were starving. To help the deer, he had cut the branches and hauled them to the edge of the deeryard. For the next couple of weeks he did this nearly every other day and brought them hay and corn from the barn as well. The food he supplied helped the remaining deer to survive.

Sam was especially happy to see Star, whom he recognized by the tiny white blaze on his forehead. He'd seen him first as a newborn fawn and later at the beaver pond, where he had helped him to escape from the dog. By now he thought of the young buck as almost an old friend.

He felt this even more strongly one afternoon when

Star approached to within twenty feet of him to feed on some of the grain that Sam had brought. The young deer looked at the boy—but he didn't seem to be afraid.

February passed, and the days grew longer. Star was still gaunt and nearly always hungry, but the food Sam brought kept him and the others alive. Day by day the temperature began to rise. One morning in mid-March Star woke to the sound of dripping water.

Each day the sights and sounds and smells of approaching spring increased. The snow gradually melted, and the deer were able to leave their winter prison. Soon they scattered over their old ranges and began to fill up on swelling buds and shoots of grass.

In the swamp frogs and toads began to trill their spring chorus. After the first gentle spring rain salamanders emerged from their winter sleeping places and made their way to the pond, to court and lay their eggs.

Budding new antlers began to push upward beneath the skin on Star's forehead. Instead of single spikes, he would have forked antlers this third summer of his life.

Tossing his head, Star went off to feed, waving his white tail behind him like a flag. He had survived the hard winter.

7

Record Buck

After the starvation winter, springtime came on with a rush. Blackbirds, their red-shouldered wings spread wide, swayed on the dried cattails in the marsh and poured out their territorial songs. Woodchucks and chipmunks left their burrows and began once again to range through the woods and fields.

By May most of the deer had scattered to their summer ranges. Each of the does eventually went off by herself to bear her fawns. The bucks banded together in bachelor groups for the summer months. Star joined forces with a companionable old buck and two other two-year-olds like himself.

Star's antlers were pushing rapidly upward and outward. Each new antler thrust up in a single stout trunk that branched into a Y-shaped prong. The hairy skin that covered the growing bone was soft as velvet. Star and his companions took care not to strike their growing antlers against rocks or tree trunks. At this stage they might easily be damaged if they received a hard blow.

During hot weather the bucks often rested at midday in a thick tangle of underbrush to avoid the heat of the sun. Sometimes they bedded down on a high, forested ridge. At dawn and dusk, and occasionally during the night, they browsed together or visited the pond to drink and cool off.

That fall, when Star's antlers had reached their full growth and hardened, he rubbed them against tree trunks and bushes to scrape away the drying velvet. His weapons ready, he sparred with the other young bucks, testing his strength. A strange, unexplainable excitement filled him as the mating season—the time of the rut—approached. The old buck grew increasingly irritable, and finally would have nothing to do with his younger companions of the summer. He drove them away from him, for he did not want any possible rivals around him.

Star was not old enough to win any mates that fall. In the contests with other young bucks, however, he began to gain the strength and experience he would need in the years to come. He was learning the ways of an adult male whitetail.

As the seasons passed, Star continued to grow and develop. He survived the hardships of the cold winter months and gained weight and strength during the warm growing seasons. Each spring and summer he grew an ever more impressive set of antlers. Each fall he became more experienced in avoiding hunters and their deadly guns. As he approached his prime of life, he became a buck almost without equal throughout the mountains of Pennsylvania.

By late summer of his seventh year Star was one of the biggest bucks in the region. He was in perfect health and condition and weighed nearly 400 pounds. His velvet-covered antlers jutted outward and forward on either side of his head, forming an imposing rack of fourteen points—seven tines on each antler. After the antlers hardened that fall, Star tested them against saplings and tree trunks. In just two days he stripped off the dried velvet in shreds. Then he sharpened and polished his bony weapons.

As the breeding season approached, his neck became swollen and massive. Now he began to challenge every buck that came near him. He was fearless these days, and few other bucks dared to fight him.

One afternoon he met a two-year-old black bear that was lumbering down a wooded path, looking for acorns. Snorting, Star pawed the ground, then lowered his head and charged at the surprised bruin, knocking him over. Squealing with pain and indignation, the young bear jumped up and ran away as fast as he could go.

In October Star began to trail every female deer whose scent he picked up, following the does' tracks with his nose to the ground. Most of the females he followed were not yet ready to mate.

One evening in early November he sighted a doe that stopped to wait for him. She wanted him to join her. Star approached slowly, his nostrils extended, the whites of his eyes showing. He held his head high, with his nose pointed skyward and his antlers laid back. When he came up to the doe, he grunted and nuzzled her side.

The doe tossed her head and walked slowly away. Star followed. As he approached her once more, he heard a loud snort behind him. Turning, he saw that another buck was approaching. His rival was almost as big as he was and had a heavy set of antlers. The buck was challenging Star for the doe.

Breathing heavily, the two big bucks faced each other, heads down, their antlers thrust forward. The hair along the ridge of each deer's back stood erect. Walking stiff-legged, they circled each other.

Suddenly Star charged his opponent, and the two came together with a loud clatter of antlers. As the bony weapons clashed, the heads of the two fighters were locked together for a moment. Twisting, Star wrenched free.

The two lunged at each other again and again. Ex-

cept for snorts and grunts and hard breathing and the sound of their antlers clashing, they fought silently. Both bucks reared up on their hind legs several times and lashed out at each other with their sharp hoofs. As the two circled and charged, the doe watched from a safe distance. Soon the small clearing in which they fought was torn up by their hoofs. All around them small bushes and saplings were broken and trampled.

Star's slightly greater weight gradually began to have its effect. He could feel the other buck yielding, being pushed slowly backward. With a quick thrust of his antlers Star ripped his rival's side. A trickle of blood appeared. Rasping with pain, the other buck backed away. Then he turned and quickly retreated.

Tossing his head in triumph, Star walked over to the doe. He had won his mate.

During the next several weeks Star won many mates—does that would bear his fawns the next spring.

8

Hunter's Moon

One afternoon in mid-November a man hidden in a clump of trees and underbrush watched as Star walked through the woods, tracking a doe. The man was an old and experienced hunter, one of the best in the state. He had heard rumors of a fabulous big buck that lived in the Blue Mountain region, and he had been scouting the area for several weeks, checking the deer trails and looking for signs of him.

As he explored the area, the hunter found rubs—trees and saplings scarred by Star's antlers—and scrapes—places where the huge buck had dug up the earth with his hoofs and antlers and left his scent. He discovered nests where Star had bedded down. He began to learn something of his habits, the trails he sometimes traveled, the areas where he browsed.

When the hunter finally caught a glimpse of Star his binoculars showed him what a magnificent animal he was. Star was the biggest buck he had ever seen in this area. His head and antlers would make an imposing trophy. The man vowed to himself that he would get that buck once the deer-hunting season began in a few days.

On the opening day of the deer season the hunter was in the woods before dawn. He headed for an area where he had found rubs and other signs left by Star and began to walk silently along one of the forest trails. Every few moments he stopped to peer about, on the alert for any movement or sound that might indicate the presence of deer. He saw tracks of does and year-

lings, but none that could have been left by a buck the size and weight of the one he was looking for.

At noon he left the trail and settled himself on a nearby log that gave him a clear view of the trail in each direction. He sat as silent and motionless as the log upon which he rested. As long as he did not move, a deer would have a hard time spotting him, as he well knew. Deer are color-blind. They locate their enemies only by movement or by hearing or smelling them.

In midafternoon a big doe came down the trail. As she passed the hunter, he heard the sound of two shots far up the slope. Someone else was up there shooting at a deer—maybe the big buck. The man winced at the thought.

The hunter didn't know it at the time, but he was right. Star had been trailing the big doe when the first shot was fired. He heard the slug whine past, a foot over his back. He bounded off the trail with a tremendous leap and headed away as fast as he could go. Another shot sounded behind him, but it, too, whined harmlessly overhead. The young hunter who had fired the shots cursed his frustration as he watched Star disappear.

As he was leaving the woods later that afternoon, the young hunter met the older one. The younger man told the other about the record buck he had shot at and missed. "He must've been eighteen points—and I missed him!" he declared ruefully. "Boy, did that buck take off when I fired at him! Must be in the next county by now."

The older hunter listened to the account with great interest but said little in reply. He, for one, was relieved to hear that the big buck was still fair game. Once a deer had been spooked like that, however, it'd probably be twice as wary during the rest of the season.

It was just as the hunter feared. During the next few days he watched and waited for Star and trailed him in many different areas. He tried every hunting trick he knew. But as he had suspected, the big buck had become increasingly wary now that hunters roamed the woods. Star spent most daylight hours hiding in thick cover, lying low in places where he would not be spotted. He usually ventured out only at night, when the woodland was clear of humans.

Lack of success only increased the hunter's determination. On the next to the last day of the season he was again in the woods before dawn. He headed for an area where two well-traveled animal trails crossed, and hid himself in a clump of bushes. Making himself as comfortable as possible, the man began a long vigil. Star, as he had previously observed, sometimes used one or the other of these trails. Perhaps he would do so today.

A light snowfall began at daybreak, but the weather was mild for late November. Chickadees called in the nearby trees, and a red squirrel sat on a limb over the hunter's head, eating pine seeds. Nothing else seemed to be moving. By midmorning the hunter had seen several does and a young buck on the trail, but they were not what he wanted. He was after the record buck. At midday he ate a sandwich and swallowed coffee from a thermos. Then he settled back once again to watch and wait.

In late afternoon the hunter glimpsed movement far down one of the trails. When he recognized Star in the distance, he felt a surge of triumph. At last! The big buck was coming up the trail toward him, head to the ground. He was not close enough yet for a shot, but getting there. The hunter waited, his rifle ready.

Star had left his hiding place that afternoon after scenting a receptive doe. He had trailed her for an hour or more but had not yet come up to her. Several times he heard far-off shots, but for the past half hour the woods had been silent. He did not see, hear, or smell anything to make him suspicious.

As Star neared the place where the hunter was hidden, the man raised his rifle and sighted it, waiting for a range at which he could not miss. His heartbeat quickened as he watched Star drawing closer, his incredible rack of antlers held proudly before him. Taking a deep breath, the hunter began to tighten his finger around the trigger.

Before he could fire, a shot suddenly rang out from some distance down the other trail, and a young buck bounded out of the woods not far from Star. Startled, the big buck leaped to one side, then took off in great, soaring bounds.

Cursing, the hunter fired two quick shots after Star as he vanished into the woods. For the second time another hunter had spoiled his chance to get the big buck. After a few moments he saw the other man hurrying down the trail after the young buck he had just fired at. He did not notice the tracks of the much larger deer.

As soon as the other had disappeared, the older hunter began to follow Star's tracks through the light snow. In a moment he saw spots of blood. One of his shots had hit the big buck after all! He would have to find him quickly, however; there was less than an hour of daylight left.

Star was more than a half mile away by this time and still running. The bullet had hit him in the right shoulder. No bones had been shattered, but the wound was painful and bleeding freely. He could not run as well as usual. For a moment he stopped to rest. He was downwind of the hunter, and a whiff of human-smell soon came his way. He was being followed.

Taking off again, Star made for a patch of swampy ground near the inlet to the beaver pond. Here a thicket of alders and other brush made an almost impenetrable barrier for either human or beast. Slowing down, Star carefully picked his way through the tangle of bushes and vines until he reached a spot where a huge old hemlock had crashed to earth. Crawling beneath the branches, he sank down and stretched his head and neck out on the ground. Ears pressed back, he lay motionless. He was as close to being invisible as he could possibly be.

But he was alert. His ears picked up every sound: a downy woodpecker hammering at a dead tree limb; a crow cawing in a distant treetop. His dark eyes took notice of every movement around him: the flick of a squirrel's tail on a tree trunk; the swaying of a branch above him when a pair of mourning doves whistled down to a landing. The sun was low in the western sky. Darkness would come very soon. Star's nostrils flared as he picked up a strong human-scent. The hunter was getting closer.

It was not long before Star saw the man approaching through the woods, gun in hand. He stopped every few moments to check the buck's tracks. Behind him

the sun was disappearing below the horizon. Soon the hunter came to the edge of the thicket in which Star lay. He peered into the forest of branches for several minutes, waiting and listening. He was no more than forty feet from Star.

The big buck's leg muscles tensed, getting ready to propel him off his bed and away if he was discovered. But he did not move. He lay waiting, as silent and still as the man searching for him.

The last light from the setting sun glimmered through the trees as he saw the hunter finally move. The man had turned away and was leaving. Star watched as the hunter disappeared through the woods. Soon it was completely dark. He had escaped one more time.

Long before dawn on the last day of the deer hunt Star left the swamp thicket and started out to find a new hiding place. Some instinct warned the big buck that he would be in danger if he remained where he was after daybreak.

A light rain was falling as he made his way slowly through the forest. The snowfall of the previous day had already disappeared. Star's shoulder wound had stopped bleeding, but the torn muscles had stiffened. Every step he took was painful. Dawn had broken by the time he reached the edge of the big woods and looked down the slope ahead of him. He wasn't far from the spot where he had been born more than seven years before.

Below the trees there was a narrow cleared strip just a few yards wide and, beyond that, a cornfield with close-set rows of seven-foot-tall stalks still standing—a rustling forest of crinkly brown leaves. After peering intently to either side, Star limped quickly across the clearing and into the corn. He headed for the middle of the stand and lay down. He would stay here today. Outside the cornfield no human could spot him.

But as Star lay there, hidden from view, the hunter was slowly following his trail. The man had come back to the swamp early in the morning. After making certain that the big buck was not in the thick cover anymore, he began to search for his tracks and finally found them in the rain-softened earth. The hoofprints pointed him in the right direction.

It was midafternoon, however, before the hunter arrived at the edge of the woods and looked down at the forest of dried cornstalks. He had lost the tracks several hundred yards back. Could the big buck be in the cornfield?

As he thought about it, he saw a young man walking up the slope toward him. He wasn't wearing a hunting outfit and did not carry a gun. The hunter assumed he must have come from the farmhouse, just visible in the distance.

Sam was nineteen years old now and was in his first year at the state university, majoring in wildlife management and biology. For years he had known that was what he wanted to do. The close contact with the wild animals around the farm and his interest in them had strengthened his decision. Looking up the slope, he remembered the fawn with the tiny white star on its forehead that he had found not far ahead when he was twelve years old. He wondered if it was still living, if it roamed the hills around his father's farm.

When he saw the hunter ahead of him, he stopped,

a frown on his face. "This farm is posted," he stated flatly. "No hunting allowed. Too risky for the livestock, for one thing."

The hunter looked at the younger man and shook his head in agreement. "I hunt only where it's legal," he assured Sam. "But there may be an injured buck in your cornfield." He told Sam that he had wounded a big buck the day before—he didn't know how badly—and had trailed it to the edge of the woods today. Perhaps it was lying dead or wounded in the cornfield.

Sam stared at the hunter for a long moment. He and his father had already cut and harvested their big field of corn next to the barn. They'd decided to hold off on this smaller field, however, until after the deer-hunting season. Too many trigger-happy hunters in the woods! "We'll go take a look," he said finally, "but no shooting!"

"Agreed," the hunter assured him quietly. For emphasis he unloaded his rifle and placed the cartridges in his pocket.

They approached the cornfield together and began to walk along its edge, peering into each row as they passed it. Nothing. As they neared the middle of the field, Sam spotted an indistinct brown mass lying some distance away, between two rows. The two began to walk slowly toward it.

Star saw them coming and lay perfectly still. Perhaps they would not see him. But they came closer and closer. Suddenly the buck sprang to his feet and stood facing the two men. Sam and the hunter stopped their advance immediately and stood motionless.

The two men and the big buck stared at one another for a long moment. With something like awe, Sam and the hunter noted Star's size, his awesome rack of antlers, his dark, shining eyes, and the tiny white star in the middle of his forehead.

At last Star snorted. Then he turned and loped away, his white flag of a tail raised behind him. His shoulder felt stiff, but he could feel the strength coursing through his veins. He left the cornfield after a few moments and headed down the slope, disappearing into a narrow strip of woodland that bordered the creek meandering through the lower meadow.

"What an animal!" Sam exclaimed, letting out a deep breath. "And he acted almost as though he recognized me." When he saw the puzzled look on the hunter's face, Sam explained how he had first seen the white-starred buck more than seven years before, when he was a tiny fawn. Later he'd seen the young buck at the beaver pond several times and had helped him to escape a big dog that was going after him. Sam also told the hunter how, during a hard winter, he had fed him. Since then he had considered the buck an old friend.

"He's not badly hurt," Sam concluded. "The hunting season ends at sunset; he'll make it!"

The hunter looked at Sam and smiled. "I think so, too," he said. "And you can rest assured that I won't go after that buck anymore. I hope he lives a good long time."

The two of them gazed at the spot where Star had entered the trees. Both knew they'd see the big buck again.

The White-tailed Deer in American History

Every year millions of hunters take to the woods all over America, hoping to bag a white-tailed deer—by far America's most abundant big-game animal. Some people hunt mainly for the pleasure they get from being in the woods and matching their skills against those of an elusive and wily quarry. Others search for trophy bucks with record racks of antlers. Nearly all of them enjoy eating the venison that is theirs after they kill a deer.

Long before European colonists came to America, the whitetail was one of the most important animals in the life of the Indians, especially those of the eastern woodlands. Indians hunted deer with bows and arrows. Venison was one of the mainstays of their diet. The Indian women used deer meat in their soups and stews. Sometimes they cut it into thin strips and dried the meat in the sun. Then they pounded it into a paste and mixed it with fat and dried berries to make pemmican—a food that could be packed in skin containers and kept fresh for weeks or months. Pemmican sustained the Indians when nothing else was available to eat. It was the food the men took with them on long hunting or raiding trips.

The deer skins were tanned and used for beds or blankets. Men wore deerskin moccasins, leggings, and jackets, and women wore deerskin dresses. Deer sinews were used in sewing and for making fishlines. Bones and antlers were fashioned into tools. Nothing was wasted.

White-tailed deer were equally important in the life of the early pioneers. They killed deer as needed throughout the year, for venison was a mainstay of their diet, too. Deer hides were tanned into soft leather for buckskin shirts, trousers, leggings, and moccasins.

No one knows how many white-tailed deer lived in North America in those precolonial days, but estimates vary from 24 to 36 million. Those figures, however, may be too high. Much of the eastern part of the continent was covered at that time with virgin forest—stands of giant evergreens or mixed hardwoods. The big trees cast a shade so dense that undergrowth had little chance beneath them. Because of this lack of edible plants, the dark depths of the big woods were poor deer habitat.

Once the pioneers had cut down the trees to build

cabins and plant crops, saplings and bushes quickly sprang up along the sunny edges of the clearings. Deer flourished on such food, and in some areas their population increased.

In time, however, many regions became so thickly settled and the forests so reduced that there wasn't enough shelter or cover for deer in them. Every year more and more settlers spread over the land, cutting down trees, clearing land, establishing farms, building towns and cities. Every year more and more deer were killed for their meat and hides.

There were practically no game laws to protect deer in those days. People figured that there was little need for them. As a result, deer meat and hides were marketed commercially in the cities, and cargoes of hides were shipped to Europe. Between 1764 and 1773 more than 2 million pounds of deerskins, for example, were passed through the single port of Savannah, Georgia. Under such pressures the whitetail gradually became scarce in many areas.

John James Audubon, the noted naturalist and bird artist, related a conversation he had with Daniel Boone during the early years of the nineteenth century. Boone told him about life in Kentucky when Boone first went there, when most of the region was "still in the hands of nature. . . .

"But ah! Sir, what a difference thirty years make in

a country. Why, at the time I was caught by Indians, you would not have walked out in any direction for more than a mile without shooting a buck or a bear. . . . But when I was left to myself on the banks of the Green River, I dare say for the last time in my life, a few signs only of deer were to be seen, and as to a deer itself, I saw none."

Uncontrolled market hunting and continued destruction of deer habitat caused the whitetail population in the United States to plunge to only 300,000 to 500,000 deer by the dawn of the twentieth century. In many regions the species had practically disappeared because of overkill and the elimination of suitable living space. Most of the surviving deer were hanging on only in remote forest or mountain areas or in wilderness swamps.

With the deer practically gone, humans finally realized that they had been taking the whitetail for granted for a long time. Game laws—regulations that protected the remaining deer and restricted hunting seasons—were passed at last.

Under management the deer began to recover. By the 1930s they had once again become plentiful, even abundant in many areas. Their old natural enemies—wolves and mountain lions—had long since disappeared, and now there was more food for deer than ever before. Selective timbering had continued to open up forested areas, allowing low bushes and young trees to spring up in such areas. The fields and clearings of an increasing number of abandoned farms sprouted new growth, too. Under such favorable conditions the whitetail population in the United States increased rapidly. Soon there were too many deer in some areas for the available habitat to support.

With protection and plenty of food, deer are very prolific. In just ten years, theoretically, the descendants of one doe and her offspring can increase to 130 animals. In one actual study a group of two bucks and four does increased to a herd of 160 animals in five years. Under protection the Pennsylvania deer herd increased from near extinction in 1900 to a population in 1930 of about 600,000—many too many deer for the available living space.

Today the whitetail ranges from southern Canada to northern South America and from the Atlantic coast almost to the Pacific in many areas. Throughout this vast range the whitetail has been divided by zoologists into about thirty different subspecies, or races. About seventeen of these are found north of the Mexican border. The largest race is the northern whitetail, which lives in the northeastern states and southern Canada; record specimens may weigh 400 pounds or more. The smallest race is the Florida Key deer, which lives on only a few of the Florida Keys and weighs just forty to eighty pounds.

The whitetail population in the United States totals 14 million or more today—a great increase over their numbers in 1900. Deer are so abundant in some places that they invade orchards, gardens, and farmers' grain-fields, causing extensive damage to crops and fruit trees. They are at home not only in wilderness areas but also in urban areas near large cities. Town and city dwellers all over the United States are often surprised to see whitetails strolling through their backyards, browsing on their shrubbery, sometimes even walking down Main Street. They cross highways in their wanderings, and nearly 150,000 deer are killed by cars every year. In one twelve-month period Pennsylvania alone had a death toll of nearly 30,000 deer killed by cars.

Today there are only two major controls on the burgeoning deer population in the United States: lack of food and hunting. During a particularly hard winter as many as 2 million deer may die of starvation and disease in regions where there are too many deer for the available food and living space. Starvation is one of nature's ways of keeping an animal's population in balance with its environment.

Hunting is the other main control of deer numbers. In the United States nearly 3 million deer are legally taken, by some 11 million hunters, during the fall deer-hunting season each year. Every state has established carefully detailed and controlled game laws and regulations governing the deer-hunting season. These regulations are usually drafted by state game biologists, then approved by the game commissioner or the legislature. If the wildlife biologists believe there are too many deer in the state for the available habitat to support, they may draw up regulations permitting the shooting of does as well as bucks, so that the deer numbers can be kept in balance with the environment. Better that way, the biologists say, than mass starvation in winter.

There are a growing number of people, however, who disagree entirely with the hunting philosophy. Animals have the same right to life as people do, they say, and they shouldn't be killed just because there are too many of them and some may starve. Hunting for food, as the Indians and pioneers did, is understandable, but killing animals just for the fun of it and as a form of recreation is not.

These people would agree with the views of Henry David Thoreau, the philosopher-writer who lived in Concord, Massachusetts. Nearly 150 years ago he observed: "Every creature is better alive than dead, men and moose and pine trees, and he who understands it aright will rather preserve its life than destroy it."

For Further Reading

The following books, although aimed primarily at adults, contain a great deal of interesting information and illustrations that should be of interest to young readers who want to learn more about the white-tailed deer and how it lives.

HOOVER, HELEN. *The Gift of the Deer*. New York: Alfred A. Knopf, 1968. A heartwarming account of the experiences the author and her husband had with deer around their log cabin home in northern Minnesota.

RAWLINGS, MARJORIE KINNAN. *The Yearling*. New York: Charles Scribner's Sons, 1938. A classic novel for readers of all ages, telling the story of a boy growing up in the backwoods of inland Florida, and the white-tailed fawn that became his pet.

RUE, LEONARD LEE, III. *The World of the White-Tailed Deer*. Philadelphia: J. B. Lippincott Co., 1962. An interesting account for the general reader of the biology and natural history of the whitetail through the four seasons of the year. Many photographs by the author.

————. *The Deer of North America.* New York: Crown Publishers, Inc., 1978. An authoritative work on the biology and natural history of all the species of North American deer, illustrated with hundreds of outstanding photographs taken by the author.

STADTFELD, CURTIS K. *The Whitetail Deer: A Year's Cycle.* New York: The Dial Press, 1975. A detailed, month-by-month account of the biology and natural history of the whitetail in Michigan throughout the year, together with the author's personal experiences and feelings about the species.

Robert McClung has always been interested in animals. At Princeton University he majored in biology, and his graduate study at Cornell was in zoology. For seven years, he was on the staff of the Bronx Zoo and later worked as an editor of natural history books. Now devoting all his time to writing, he is the author of *Rajpur: Last of the Bengal Tigers, Gorilla, Last Wild Worlds,* and many other critically acclaimed nonfiction titles. He has been the recipient of the Eva L. Gordon Award of the American Nature Study Society.

Irene Brady was born in Ontario, Oregon, and received a Bachelor of Professional Arts degree from the Oregon College of Art in Ashland. She is the author of several books, including *America's Horses and Ponies,* and has illustrated numerous others, including *Gorilla, Rajpur: Last of the Bengal Tigers,* and *Animal Baby-Sitters.*

DATE DUE			
MAY 0 6 1998			